What Does the
PRESIDENT Do?

David J. Jakubiak

PowerKiDS
press

New York

For Aiden

Published in 2010 by The Rosen Publishing Group, Inc.
29 East 21st Street, New York, NY 10010

First Edition

Editor: Amelie von Zumbusch
Book Design: Julio Gil
Photo Researcher: Jessica Gerweck

Photo Credits: Cover, pp. 5, 18 Mandel Ngan/AFP/Getty Images; p. 6 Jamie Squire/Getty Images; p. 9 Wirelmage/Getty Images; p. 10 White House/Getty Images; p. 13 Ralf-Finn Heston-Pool/ Getty Images; p. 14 Scott J. Ferrell/Congressional Quarterly/Getty Images; p. 17 Dirck Halstead/ Time Life Pictures/Getty Images; p. 21 Kean Collection/Getty Images.

Library of Congress Cataloging-in-Publication Data

Jakubiak, David J.
  What does the president do? / David J. Jakubiak.
      p. cm. — (How our government works)
  Includes index.
  ISBN 978-1-4358-9357-3 (library binding) — ISBN 978-1-4358-9810-3 (pbk.) —
ISBN 978-1-4358-9811-0 (6-pack)
  1. Presidents—United States—Juvenile literature. 2. United States—Politics and government—
Juvenile literature. I. Title.
  JK517.J35 2010
  352.230973—dc22
                                    2009027404

Manufactured in the United States of America

CPSIA Compliance Information: Batch #WW10PK: For Further Information contact Rosen Publishing, New York, New York at 1-800-237-9932

CONTENTS

THE BIGGEST JOB IN THE LAND

On January 20, 2009, Barack Obama became the forty-fourth president of the United States. Looking over a huge crowd, Obama announced, "Everywhere we look, there is work to be done."

Americans look to their president to fix many problems. After a flood or storm, a president can help get people aid. As commander in chief, the president can send troops to war. If a kind of animal is in danger of dying out, the president can find ways to keep that animal safe. Being president also requires talking with reporters, meeting with other government leaders, and traveling the world as the face of the United States.

An American president is the official head of the U.S. military. Here, President Obama (right) is meeting with soldiers who have been serving their country in Iraq.

In different places, people cast their votes in different ways. Some fill out paper ballots, as these voters are doing. Others use voting machines or special computers.

HOW PRESIDENTS ARE CHOSEN

Every four years, people across the country stay up late on a Tuesday night in November. It is Election Day, and voters are waiting to find out who will be the next president of the United States!

Each state has a set number of votes in the electoral college. These votes are based on a state's number of senators and congressional representatives.

Millions of Americans cast a **ballot** for president. Some people vote at local schools or churches. Others vote by mail. After the voting ends, the counting begins. Election results are reported one state at a time. As winners are announced in each state, **candidates** gain electoral votes. A candidate needs 270 electoral votes to win the presidency.

THE FIRST DAY IN OFFICE

Presidents are elected in November but do not take office until January. When a new president has been elected, the period after the election begins a transition. This is when the president's team is built.

On Inauguration Day, the president takes office. First, the president must take the presidential **oath**. In the oath, the president promises to follow the U.S. **Constitution**. Inauguration Day is often honored by a parade and by parties called inaugural balls. Inaugural balls began with President James Madison in 1809. In 1997, President Bill Clinton had 14 balls for his second inauguration!

On his inauguration day, in 1977, President Jimmy Carter (center) chose to walk rather than drive in the parade honoring him. His wife and daughter walked along with him.

The United States and the Soviet Union were enemies for many years. Reagan (right) and Gorbachev (left) tried to settle problems between the countries peacefully.

A POWERFUL WORLD LEADER

The world watches everything a president does. As the head of state, the president decides how our country will work with other countries. Presidents can reach out to other leaders to solve problems. This can mean working with friendly countries, called allies. It also means trying to work with unfriendly countries. The president has the power to make **treaties**, too.

In 1986, President Ronald Reagan flew to Iceland to meet with Mikhail Gorbachev, the leader of the **Soviet Union**. The two leaders agreed to reduce the number of some of their most powerful **weapons**. The agreement showed that two unfriendly nations could sometimes work together.

GETTING HELP FROM THE CABINET

Presidents deal with everything from schools to national parks. The president is the head of the executive branch. This part of the **federal** government directs how laws are carried out. It has 15 departments, each dealing with one subject. For example, the Department of Health and Human Services makes sure that food is safe, among other things.

The vice president is the next person in command after the president. If a president dies or cannot lead, the vice president must be ready to take over.

The heads of these departments also advise the president. Along with the vice president, they make up the cabinet. Presidents meet often with their cabinets to talk about important matters.

Here, Vice President Joe Biden (left) and President Obama (center) visit a school with Arne Duncan (right). Duncan is the head of the Department of Education.

Each year, the president reports to Congress in a speech called the State of the Union. Here, President George W. Bush gives his fourth State of the Union address.

MAKING LAWS WITH CONGRESS

In the early 2000s, President George W. Bush wanted to change education laws. However, a president cannot make laws alone. Bush worked with members of **Congress** to create the No Child Left Behind Act. The law requires testing in reading and math for many students.

The president can veto, or turn down, a bill. However, a vetoed bill can still become law if two-thirds of the members of both houses of Congress vote for it.

Laws begin in Congress as bills. Congress has two parts, or houses. They are the Senate and the House of Representatives. If both houses of Congress pass a bill, it goes to the president. If the president signs the bill, it becomes a law.

CHOOSING THE COURT

The president works with all branches of government. Presidents help shape the **Supreme Court** by picking people to fill openings there. Whom a president picks can send a strong message. In 1967, President Lyndon Johnson was fighting for equal treatment for Americans of all races. He picked Thurgood Marshall to join the Supreme Court. Marshall became the court's first African-American member.

The Supreme Court is made up of nine judges, called justices. The justices decide if laws have been correctly used. For example, in 1954, the Court said that having different schools for children of different races went against the Constitution.

In 1994, President Bill Clinton (right) picked Stephen Breyer (left) to fill an open spot on the Supreme Court. Clinton called Breyer an "outstanding" judge.

Over the years, several children have called the White House home. Today, President Obama's daughters, Sasha (left) and Malia (second from right), live there.

A BIG HOUSE AND A PRIVATE JET

The job of president comes with a big house, called the White House. The White House has 132 rooms, 35 of which are bathrooms. It has a movie theater, a jogging track, and a vegetable garden. It also has tight security, including a system that tracks movement on the grounds.

Many presidents have had dogs and cats at the White House. President Calvin Coolidge even had a raccoon named Rebecca. The president and his raccoon took evening walks together.

The president also has a private **retreat** at Camp David, in the mountains of Maryland. On the road, the president rides in a special limousine. In the air, the president flies on *Air Force One*. This jet has two kitchens that can fix meals for 100 people.

PRESIDENT ABRAHAM LINCOLN

Throughout history, presidents have faced the big questions of their time. For example, President Abraham Lincoln dealt with slavery and tried to hold the **Union** together. Today, he is considered one of our greatest presidents.

In Lincoln's time, most African Americans in the South were slaves. The country was growing, too. As states joined, people argued about whether they should allow slavery there. Lincoln was against slavery. After his election in 1861, 11 Southern states left the Union. However, Lincoln fought a war to keep the Union together. He also signed a law that freed slaves in the South. Lincoln managed to reunite the country and end slavery.

Lincoln (center) visited several battlefields. At one, he promised "government of the people, by the people, for the people, shall not perish from the earth."

OUR NEWEST PRESIDENT

Barack Obama made history when he was elected president in 2008. He became our first African-American president. Obama regularly meets with his cabinet to study health care and education. He has worked with Congress to help families hold on to their homes in bad times. He also met with world leaders to talk about **global warming**.

The presidency has been filled by different kinds of leaders from across the country. Some presidents grew up on farms, some in cities. They have often held very different ideas about what the president should do. If you were the president, what would you do?

GLOSSARY

ballot (BA-lut) A form that people fill in to vote.

candidates (KAN-dih-dayts) People who run in an election.

Congress (KON-gres) The part of the U.S. government that makes laws.

Constitution (kon-stih-TOO-shun) The basic rules by which the United States is governed.

federal (FEH-duh-rul) Having to do with the central government.

global warming (GLOH-bul WARM-ing) A gradual increase in how hot Earth is. It is caused by gases that are let out when people burn fuels such as gasoline.

oath (OHTH) A promise.

retreat (rih-TREET) A safe place to hide or get away.

Soviet Union (SOH-vee-et YOON-yun) A former country that reached from eastern Europe across Asia to the Pacific Ocean.

Supreme Court (suh-PREEM KORT) The highest court in the United States.

treaties (TREE-teez) Official agreements, signed and agreed upon by each party.

Union (YOON-yun) The joining of different states into one nation.

weapons (WEH-punz) Objects or tools used to hurt or kill.

INDEX

WEB SITES

Due to the changing nature of Internet links, PowerKids Press has developed an online list of Web sites related to the subject of this book. This site is updated regularly. Please use this link to access the list:
www.powerkidslinks.com/hogw/pres/